A Quiet Beauty

*Images of the Blue Ridge
in Words and Photos*

Patricia S. Taylor Edmisten

A Quiet Beauty
Copyright © 2019
All rights reserved. This book or any portion thereof may not be reproduced or used in any manner whatsoever without the express written permission of the publisher except for the use of brief quotations in a book review.
Printed in the United States of America
First Printing, 2019

ISBN: 9781710053746

Also by the Author:

Nicaragua Divided: La Prensa and the Chamorro Legacy

Translation, Prologue, Afterword, the Autobiography of María Elema Moyano: The Life and Death of a Peruvian Activist

The Mourning of Angels (novel set in Peru)

The Treasures of Pensacola Beach (poetry and photos)

Wild Women with Tender Hearts (Peace Corps Writers' Award for Poetry)

Kennedy's Children (Screenplay)

A Longing for Wisdom: One Woman's Conscience and her Church

Water Skiing on the Amazon

*For family and friends who have loved
"Montezuma's Reward"*

JEWELWEED

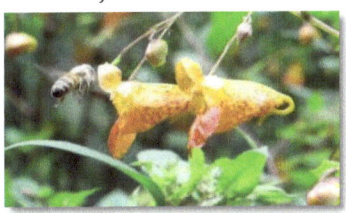

Contents

Introduction: Ida's Ghost   2

Spring

Opening the Farmhouse	7
It Takes Two Weeks	8
Breathing Space	9
Siempre Verde, Always Green	9
Weeding	10
Mountain Deluge	10
Granddaddy and the Snake	12
Lavender	19

Summer

Rosa rugosa rubra	21
The White Rocker	22
Ralph	23
Cool Dogs	26
Sunflowers	26
A Prayer from Water and Stone	27
Beauty has this Effect	29
The God Particle	30
Creation	32

Fall

You Could Die on Such a Day	40
Autumn	41

Fall Break	42
Autumn Rose	42
Smokey's Dying	42
A Gnarled Apple Tree	43
Gold	43
The Sun on my Back	44
My Heart Stretches	45
From Christmas Trees to Chestnut Trees	46
Migration South	50

Winter

Snowy Morning	55
The Yellow House Coat	56
Winter a Quieter Beauty	57
About the Author	61
Acknowledgement	62

You see, I want a lot.
Maybe I want it all:
the darkness of each endless fall,
the shimmering light of each ascent.

So many are alive who don't seem to care.
casual, easy, they move in the world
as though untouched.

But you take pleasure in the faces
Of those who know they thirst.
You cherish those
Who grip you for survival.

You are not dead yet, it's not too late
To open your depths by plunging into them
And drink in the life
That reveals itself quietly there.

>Rainer Maria Rilke
>*Book of Hours*, I, 14.
>Translated from the German by
>Anita Barrows and Joanna Macy

Spring

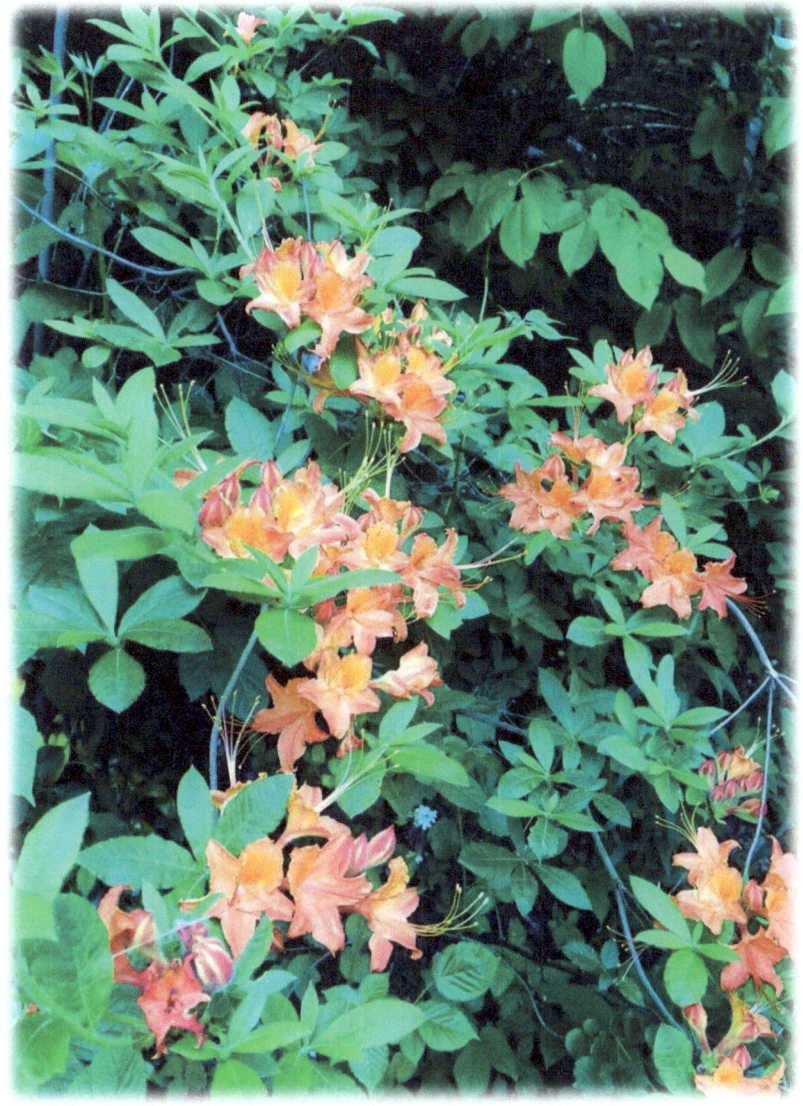

Native Flame Azalea

Introduction: Ida's Ghost

My husband Joe and I had only been married one month when we packed the car and headed for his mountain farmhouse in Montezuma, NC. "Montezuma's Reward" was built in 1886 and is located about forty minutes south of Boone, two miles south of Newland, the county seat, and two miles west of Linville in the northwestern corner of the state, not far from the Tennessee border. The elevation is about 4,000 feet. My only child, a teen-aged son, now in a blended family of six children, accompanied us, along with his best friend.

Before it became Montezuma, our village had been known as Bull Scrape. You'll understand why, then, in the late 1800s, villagers decided to rename their community after the Aztec emperor who defended his territory against Spanish invaders in the early 1500s. More than three centuries later, in 1847, during the Mexican-American war, North American Marines and men of the U.S. Army, invaded Mexico and defeated Santa Ana's troops. That battle is still commemorated in "The Halls of Montezuma," the Marine Hymn. I figure that Bull Scrapers were more familiar with that battle than with the emperor after whom they named their village.

Joe, who had grown up on a large farm in Boone, had bought the farmhouse and surrounding two and one-half acres, along with the rights to a spring. The spring, according to the original deed, forms part of the headwaters of the North Toe

River. "Toe" is a shortening of the Indian name "Estatoe," used to identify one of their early trade routes. The waters from the North Toe join those of the Nolichucky, Tennessee, Ohio, and, ultimately, the Mississippi River before emptying into the Gulf of Mexico.

Joe later purchased an additional fifteen acres of wooded mountainside that rises behind the house. At the time he had his own ecological consulting firm in Pensacola, Florida, and I was teaching at the University of West Florida in the same city.

During the years before we married, Joe had leased the farmhouse to a woman who fancied herself an English earth mother, given the stacks of British house and garden-type magazines I found. There were, however, only weeds in the garden plot. In fact, our would-be Brit took off leaving the place a shambles.

That first night, exhausted from sweeping, scrubbing, wiping, brushing, shaking, and airing, I collapsed into bed alongside Joe. Each boy took a bedroom upstairs. At about 2:00 a.m., I awoke to the sound of wind in the stairwell next to our bedroom. It was a rushing, frantic, angry sound, as if it were unsure of which direction to take, up or down. Then I heard the tremulous voice of my otherwise confident son: "Mom, is that you?" He, too, had heard the wind. He called again, this time more urgently, "Mom?"

By this time my adrenaline was surging. Not wanting to appear the stereotypical wife who nudges her husband and whispers, "darling, I hear a noise, would you check it out?" I pushed the covers aside, grabbed the bedside flashlight, and slowly ascended the stairs. The "wind," that I could still hear but not feel, had subsided by the time I reached the top. I checked on my son, reassuring him that all was well. His friend slept soundly. Back in bed, I reminded myself that I didn't believe in ghosts, but what else could have caused that sound? All the windows were closed. (Thirty-six years later, the story has become part of our family lore, but the version depends upon who tells the story.)

    Maybe it was Ida who did the haunting, the grandmother who died in the house that her husband Wilbur had built for her. Together they raised four strapping sons and two dutiful daughters. I can attempt a reconstruction of her day based on the life of my heroic mother-in-law, Nellie Mae, who raised five sons and one daughter with her husband Walter, a proud, honorable farmer. Like Nellie, I'm guessing that Ida's workday began at 5:00 a.m., even on frigid mornings when the only heat came from the wood cook stove. Her husband and children needed to eat well so every morning Ida prepared their eggs, sausage, gravy and biscuits. When times were good they had coffee.

    In summer she canned apple sauce, green beans, tomatoes, corn, vegetable beef soups (if a cow had been recently slaughtered and butchered). She also made and canned her own sausage made from their own pigs. All these she stored in the root cellar that still stands on our land, the lower third buried in soil that keeps the preserved food cool in the summer and prevents freezing in the winter.

No sooner were the breakfast dishes washed and put away than Ida, with the help of her daughters, had the noon dinner underway. Throughout even the coldest winter months the family had enough to eat. Ida finally got running water when the spring house was added just off the kitchen. She and her daughters no longer had to carry water from the branch that flowed through their land. Instead, gravity carried it underground through a pipe from the spring high above them right into the spring house where a trough held the icy water that the family used for cooking, bathing, or for storing perishables like milk and butter.

Twenty years after we took over the farmhouse I was surprised by a visit from three women who lived in the same valley. They were Ida's now mature granddaughters who had spent much of their childhoods in our house. They asked if they could take a look around. They squealed with delight as they returned to the rooms they had known so well, remembering how they had hunkered down under multiple quilts in the winter to keep warm, and how the snow would blow through the crevices between the window and frame, allowing tiny drifts to form in the inside corners of the sills.

When I recollect our first night in Montezuma's Reward, I do believe that Ida was checking us out. Peeved at the intruders, maybe even outraged, she recognized that we had found her home a comforting place to live, and that we posed no threat to her memory or that of her family. May she rest in peace.

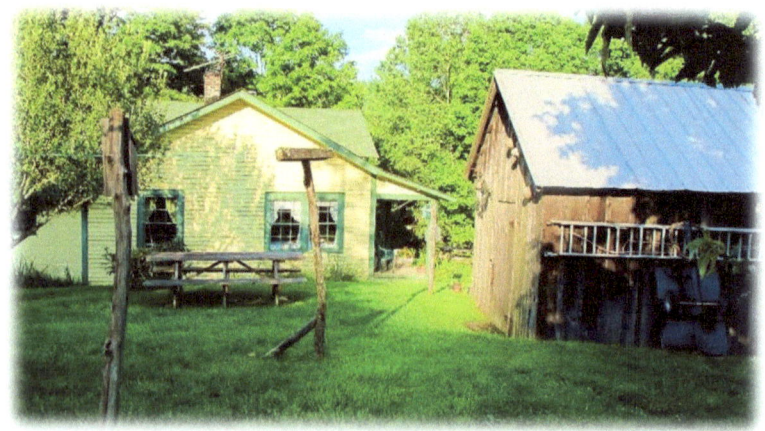

Montezuma's Reward

Opening the Farmhouse

We were opening the old farmhouse that had been shuttered for eight months. I was sweeping out cobwebs and brushing the dead hornets from the windowsills. Joe was plowing the garden site. While changing bed linens, I noticed a hole in the center of a green blanket, not a neat hole, but one with fuzzy edges, as if it had been gnawed. In the middle of the hole moved a thin, wiry tail. Shit.

I opened the window and called Joe. He'd know how to remove the rodent. With Joe at my side, I flung back the covers. She was a tiny field mouse, and she was nursing six thimble-sized babies. I know I'm guilty of assigning human qualities to an animal, but I swear she looked at us in sheer terror. Why not when she and her young were so vulnerable?

Joe told me to get his leather work gloves "What are you going to do?" I asked. "Kill them," he said. "Can't we put a basket down on top of them and release them outside?" I pleaded.

Not waiting for us to act, mama mouse hauled her young, mouths still clamped to her tits, down the back of the mattress and into the hole in the wall. Relieved, I washed and patched the blanket.

It Takes Two Weeks

It takes two weeks for my city soul to
light up with the fireflies in the black woods.
It takes two weeks for my heart to sing
with the warbler's arpeggio in the morning,
It takes two weeks for the white blossoms
on thorny stems to become the tight green buttons
that will become succulent blackberries,
Mogen David-sweet.

It takes two weeks for my soul to laugh
with the spring's cold, clear water,
captured from subterranean crannies
and two weeks before
the wild turkey crosses my path,
the fox startles me,
the corn breaks through the soil,
and the neighbor's dog claims us.

It takes two weeks before my
irregular heart beats with nature.

Breathing Space

Alone on the farm,
A hummingbird drones
inches from my face.
Its vulnerable ruby throat
swallows iridescent iris dew.
I breathe deeply
while feathery breezes
caress my needy cheeks.

Siempre Verde, Always Green

Bold lilac buds,
portents of fragrant, violet pleasure.
Valiant daffodils,
dewey-fresh scent of spring.
Intrepid forsythia,
safer in an Oriental vase,
all taken unaware by winter's last stand.
Oh, that I could rebound from sixty winters,
eager for the gifts of spring,
siempre verde, always green.

Weeding

Her back aches.
Still she positions cracked fingers
with dirt-packed nails
around the roots,
trailing them,
encircling them,
probing beneath them
in the moist, fecund soil,
careful not to break them.
Weeds could sprout anew,
sending spiky shoots and ominous leaves
that shade precious buds from the sun.

Mountain Deluge

For ten days and ten nights
Rain, like sweet antiseptic
Cleansed us of greed
Purged us of self-interest
Flooded us with concern for each other
Swept away our prejudices
Eroded our righteousness
Ministered to our parched souls
Bathed us in hope
Blessed us with insights
Anointed us with second chances

Baptized us with new life
Drenched us with confidence

Sprinkled good works
Dampened our anger
Doused our resentments
Surged over our cities
Flowed from our hearts
Trickled from our tongues
Extinguished the hatred
Moistened our will
Poured forth renewal
Gushed forth kindness
Washed us in love.

The ark is safe.

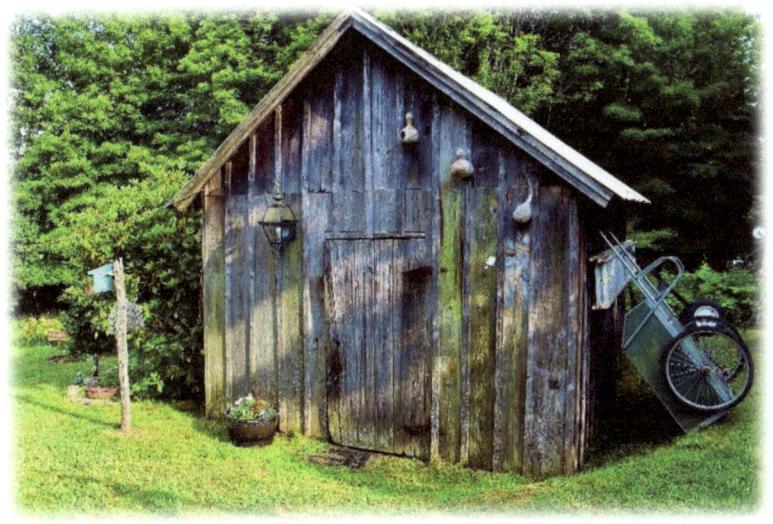

Wood Shed

Granddaddy and the Snake

I was searching for a classical music station on our old FM radio, moving the tuner slowly, listening hard to find one of the few public radio channels we sometimes can bring into our farmhouse when I saw its head. I was sitting on the worn cocktail table in front of the radio, and the snake's head and upper body were right next to my left foot.

"Oh, that Joe," I thought "He must be pulling a prank on me. It's a rubber snake." But then I thought I saw its head move just the slightest "Nah, I must be imagining things," I told myself. Not taking any chances, however, I slowly got up and backed away. Returning with a flashlight, and standing at a cautious distance, I saw that the snake was real. It was brown; its head was small and just a little wider than his body that stood erect as if ready to strike. The snake's eyes followed the light as if hypnotized.

Joe was hoeing the garden when I called him. After surveying the situation, he told me to keep the flashlight on the snake's head. And what comes next introduced me to a whole new side of my husband. While the snake stared at the light, Joe's hand came up from behind and grabbed its head. Then he pulled, and he pulled, and he pulled until the snake's whole six feet or more were coiled around Joe's arm.

"Joe, please, get that thing out of here. Take it as far away from the house as possible," I pleaded. Apparently, the snake still had some leeway because, in an instant, it turned its head and bit Joe's hand. Stalwart Joe continued toward the woods where he flung the snake as far as he could.

Although Joe paid it no mind, I was concerned about the bite and put pressure on the small wound to force out blood and insisted that Joe run his hand under the tap. He checked his snake books and decided that it was a rat snake:

"A medium to large constrictor found throughout much of the northern hemisphere. Generally thought to be non-venomous, it is an old-world species that has been found to have small amounts of venom, negligible when transferred by bites to humans. Their diet consists primarily of rodents and birds."

This one must have squeezed under our screen door.

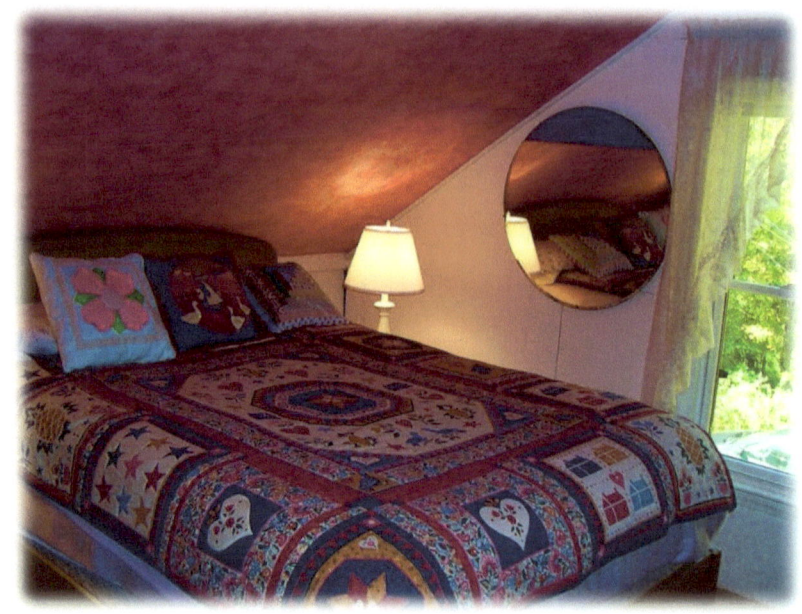

The Rose Room

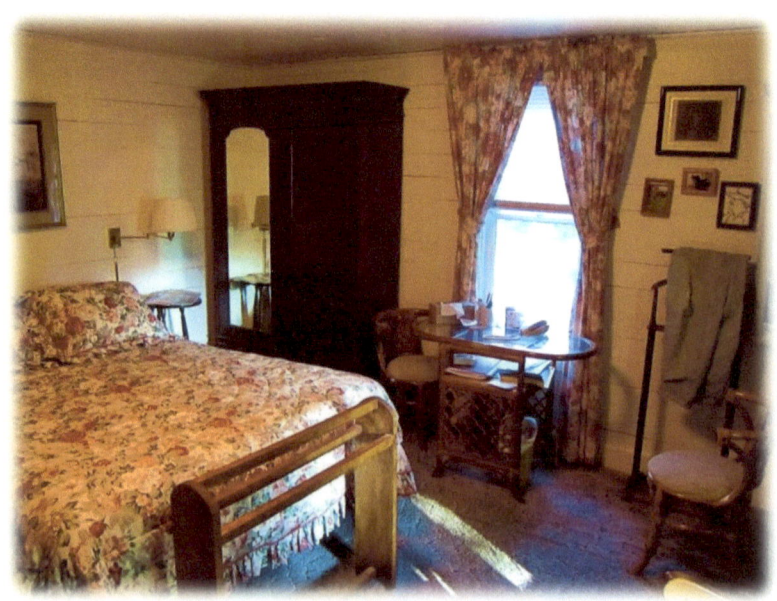

The Master Bedroom

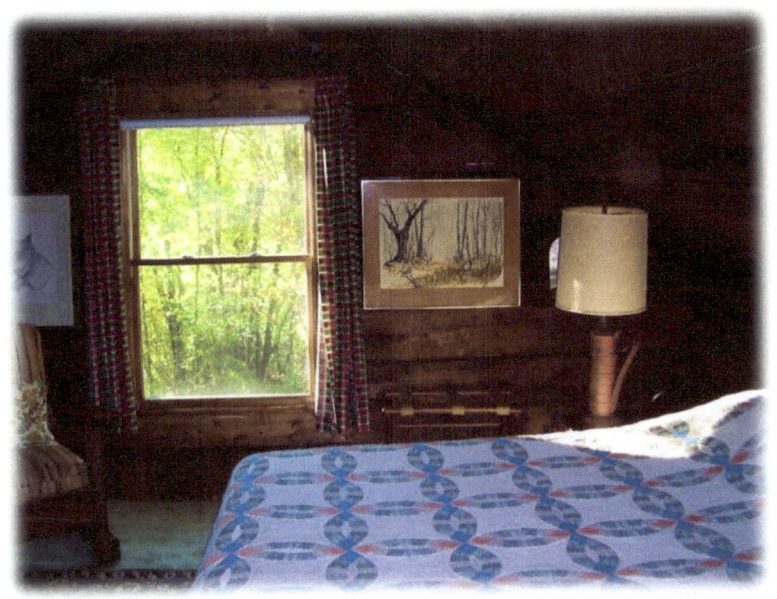

The Barnboard Room

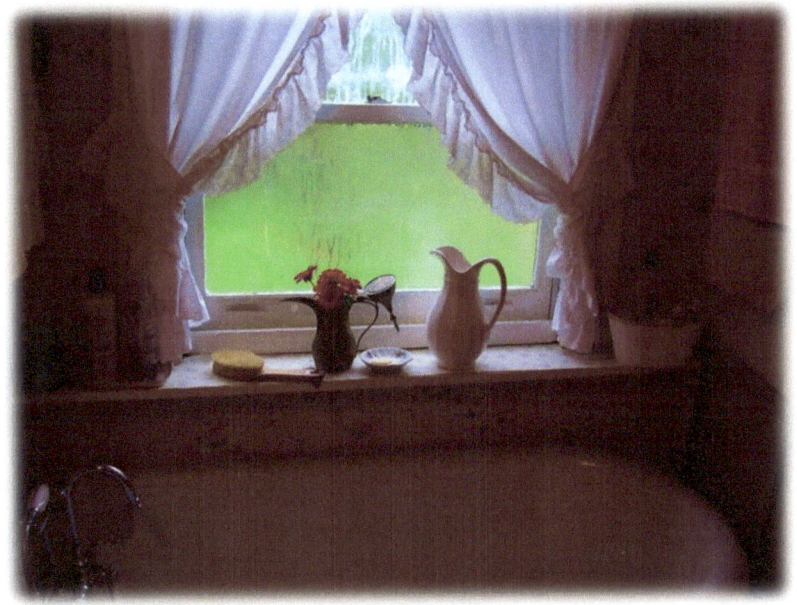

The Bath

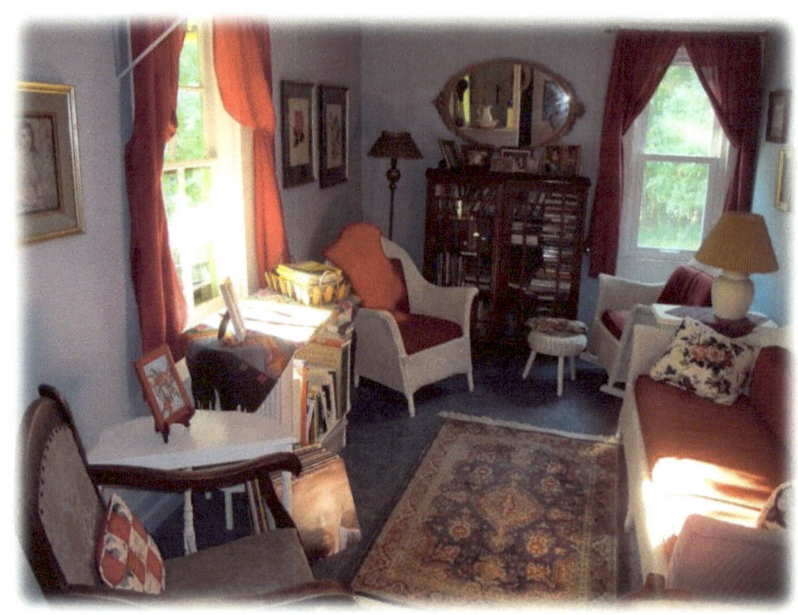

The Parlor

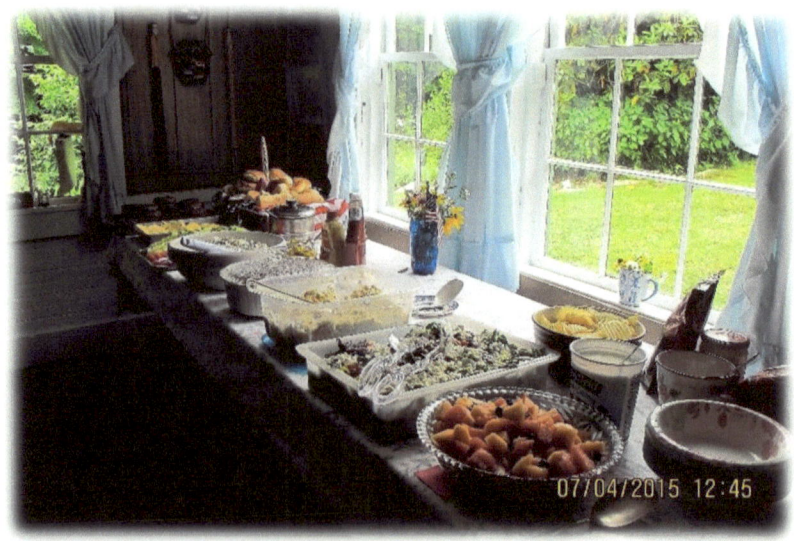

Fourth of July

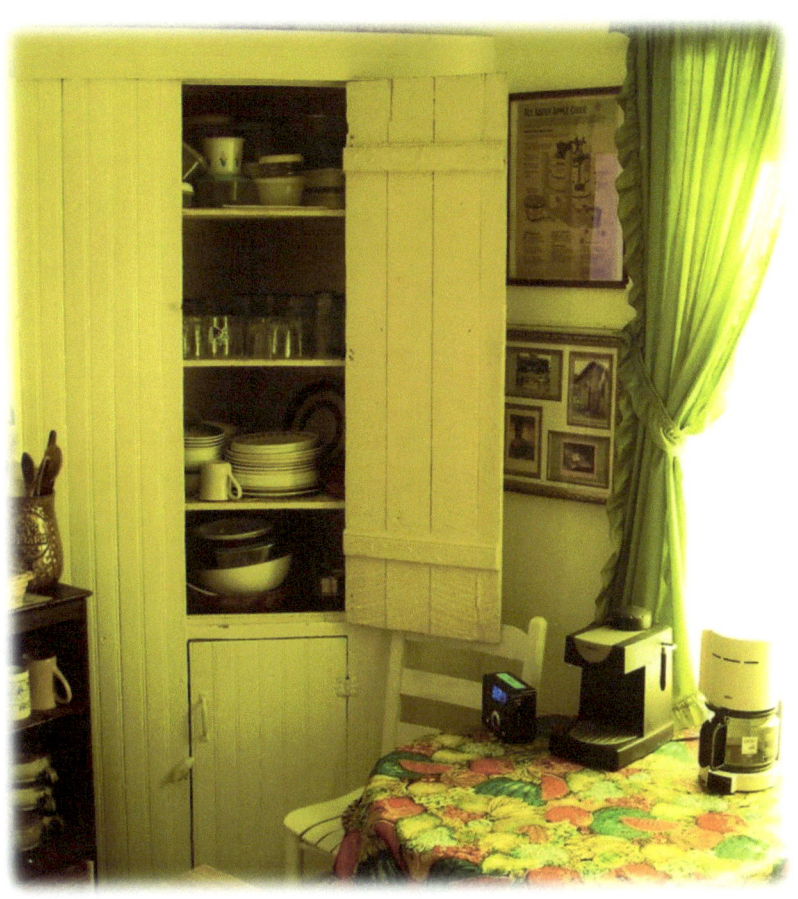

The Corner Kitchen Cabinet

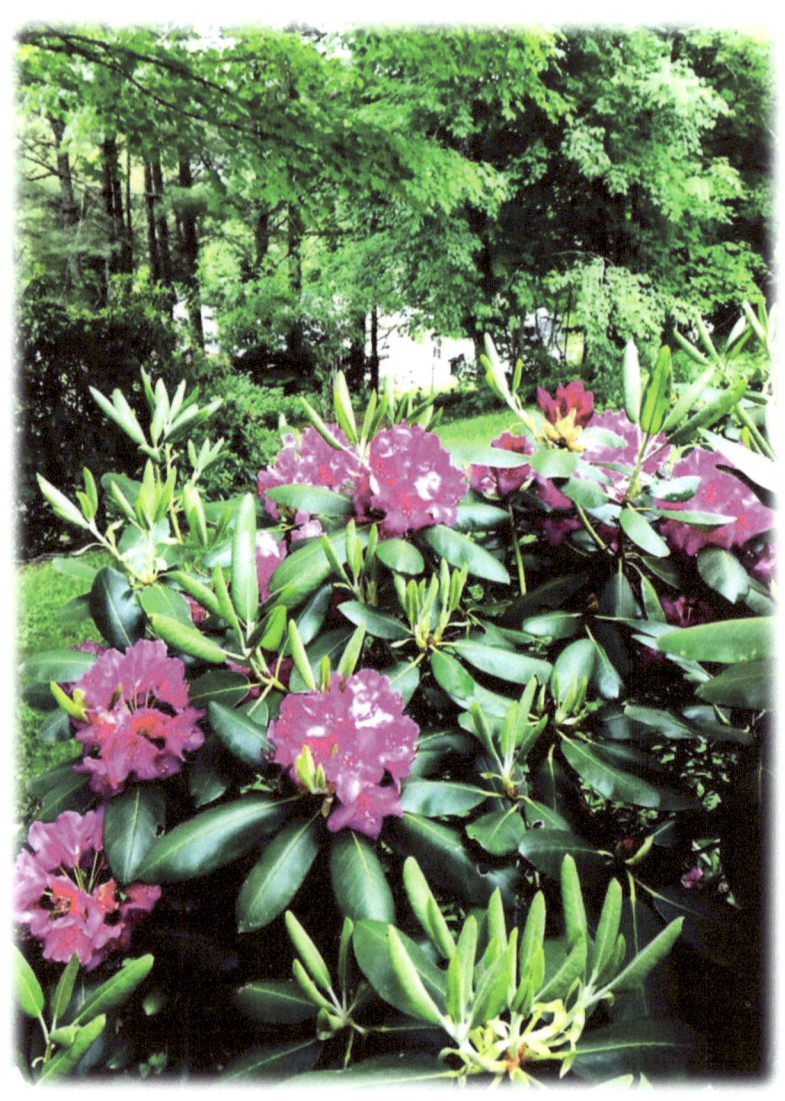

Catawba Rhododendron

Lavender

At dawn, a quiet quilt of lavender sky
becomes a royal canopy for fragrant lilacs.
The orange gladiola shouts,
"Please, embrace me too, calm me. I'm
tired of standing apart, making a statement.
I want to be like you —
lavender."

Summer

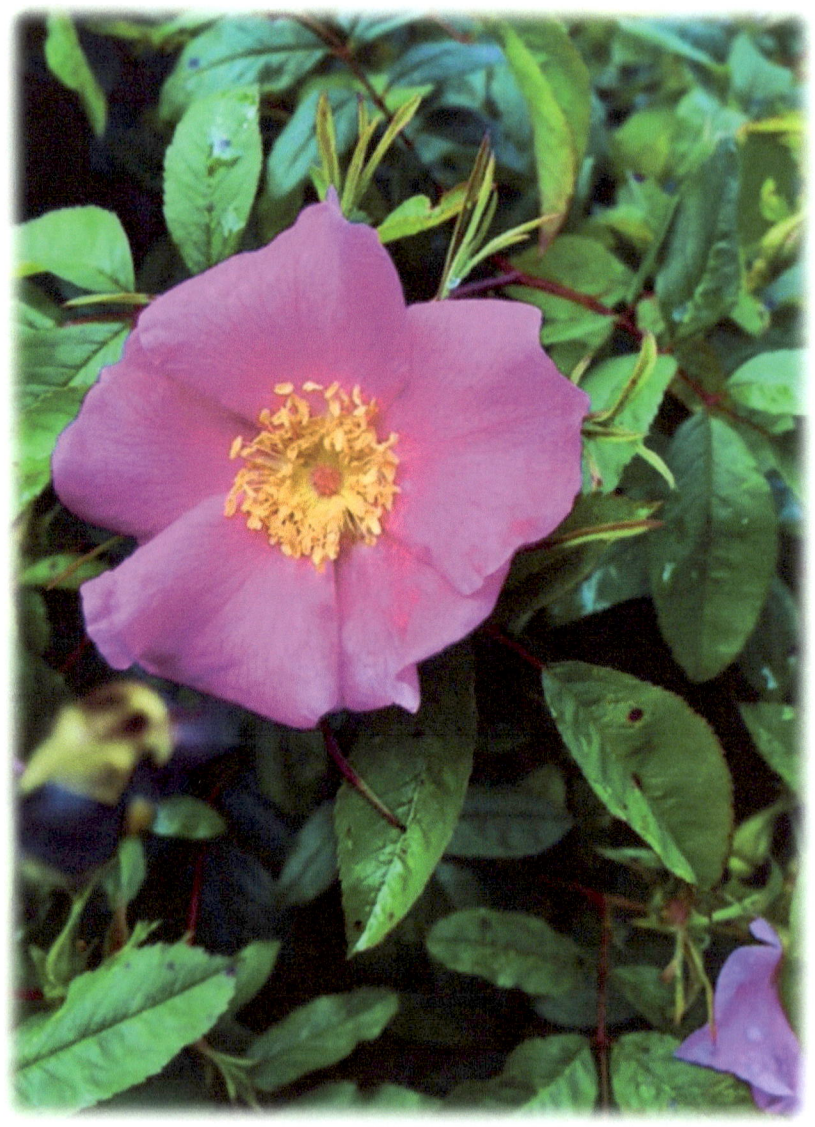

Rosa rugosa rubra

Rosa rugosa rubra

Like the name of
an Italian actress,
more lovely than Sophia Loren,
they are after you.

Drunk on your fragrance,
they enter you, one after another,
imbibing your nectar.
You open your tender parts to all.

They take their pleasure
and leave with your pollen
to fertilize another
lovely *Rosa rugosa rubra.*

The White Rocker

I sit in the white rocker
on the side porch,
wrapped in a colorful Afghan
made by a lady older than I.

A female hummingbird sips
from the feeder, while her wings
flap seventy times a second.
I marvel at her staunch heart.

The yellow lilies reach for the sun
as St. Francis, with a cement dove in his hand,
and a real one on his head,
tells them they are finely arrayed.

Two young rabbits cavort in the grass.
Chipmunks stuff their jowls with bird seed
or a single chestnut they carry
to their winter pantries.
I am both guest and resident in this peaceful world.

Ralph SlimFast

Ralph was a trim, medium-sized, tan mutt with the prettiest eyes and lashes you've ever seen on a dog. You knew that when he looked at you that he loved only you. He knew your moods, when you wanted to play, when you needed a quiet companion, and when you needed a therapeutic wet snout near your face along with a soft little moan to prove his sincerity. My husband cradled him like a baby. Ralph would nestle into his chest and look up into my husband's eyes as if there were no other love.

We took for granted that Ralph would always find us shortly after our June arrival at our mountain farmhouse in Montezuma, NC. (We call our place "Montezuma's Reward" to distinguish it from the intestinal ailment.) After settling in, we might wake to find Ralph asleep on our porch or he'd surprise us during the cocktail hour on the side porch, as the sun was slanting through the maple grove, putting a blush on the tomatoes.

Two of our grandchildren were visiting during one of Ralph's summer adoptions of our family. He loved their attention and enjoyed spreading out over their small laps. He made it clear, however, that, during their visits, he would not be giving up his usual pastime of chasing rabbits and groundhogs. He could still give our family the affection we craved while living up to the full name we gave him as a puppy: "Ralph SlimFast," after the diet drink that was invented some forty years ago. Like many dogs raised in rural North Carolina, Ralph was free-range. He had his home base, but he also had a stable of loving families scattered about the area who thought that Ralph loved only them.

While the grandchildren and I were having lunch one day, we heard a faint yelping. Sophie went into the family room and reported that the sound was coming from under the house. It was Ralph. A rabbit could navigate all the tunnels and burrows under our old farmhouse, dug by groundhogs throughout generations, but a dog like Ralph could get stuck. I gave Sophie a hot dog and asked her to go outside to the opening through which I thought Ralph had entered. She called to him trying to get him to back out if he couldn't turn around. No such luck.

Vincent remembered that we had a circular opening around a pipe under the kitchen sink that was covered by a board made to fit the opening so that plumbing emergencies might be accessible. Removing the board, I stuck my head near the hole and called to Ralph. His yelping sounded more like human crying now. And then, as if propelled by a rocket, his head burst through the hole, but it was too small for the rest of him. We spoke baby talk to soothe him, and I caressed his head. Yes, we could have tried to make the hole bigger with a small saw, but there was no way Ralph would have backed up enough to give us the leeway we would need. In desperation, Ralph thrust his shoulder through the hole, like a baby exhausted from a long labor. Now

I was able to pull the rest of him out from under the sink, like a magician pulls a rabbit out of a hat. Ralph never stayed around to say thanks, but my grandson said, "I bet you're the only grandmother who has ever pulled a dog out from under her kitchen sink."

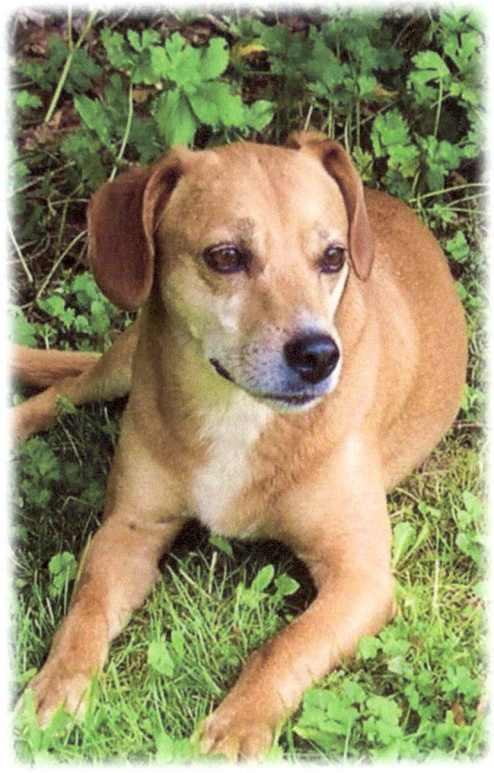

Ralph

Cool Dogs

Walking toward the drug store on
this warm afternoon, I noticed a tiny,
white-haired matron in the parking lot.
She was wearing plaid Bermudas and a tidy
white shirt tucked into her elastic waist band.
She left the engine running, and, with a second
key, locked two miniature French poodles
into her over-sized red SUV. The vehicle became
their PRD, personal refrigeration device.
Returning back to my Compact Prius
(smaller than the Prius),
I scrounged for a piece of paper.
On a bank deposit envelope I wrote,
"Remember Climate Change?"
I tucked the paper under her windshield wiper.
The air is going to the dogs, I thought.

Sunflowers

Vanguard of sun's glory —
you boisterous, blinding bunch.
Virasol, sun turners,
you humiliate me
with your dazzle.
You dazzle me.
You just dazzle me.

A Prayer from Water and Stone

What would my prayer be if I whispered thanks
to the Creator for this pure stream whose gulps
and gurgles clear my mind of resentment and fear?
The water tumbles down the mountain, over rocks
and through marsh to be captured below
in a rusty pipe so folks not be harmed
after a heavy rain.

"Let not this beauty pass."

Before me, a pool of cold spring water.
Long-legged water striders propel themselves
across the surface toward debris bits
mistaking them for edible morsels.
They water-walk in a circle
returning to the same speck
like we who repeat the same mistakes over and
over.

"Help me change my ways."

On the banks purple asters and goldenrod
consort with yellow and orange jewelweed
known also as touch-me-nots
for the tightly coiled springs their pods hold.
Children scream when the seeds spray
at the slightest touch of their fingers.

"Lord, may I share my best with this hurting
world."

I climb a path alongside five waterfalls
before reaching a solitary place.
For millions of years the water has flowed
from some unknown source,
boring tunnels through boulders,
leaving polished holes in the rock
where salamanders and crayfish hide,

"Help me live well my remaining years."

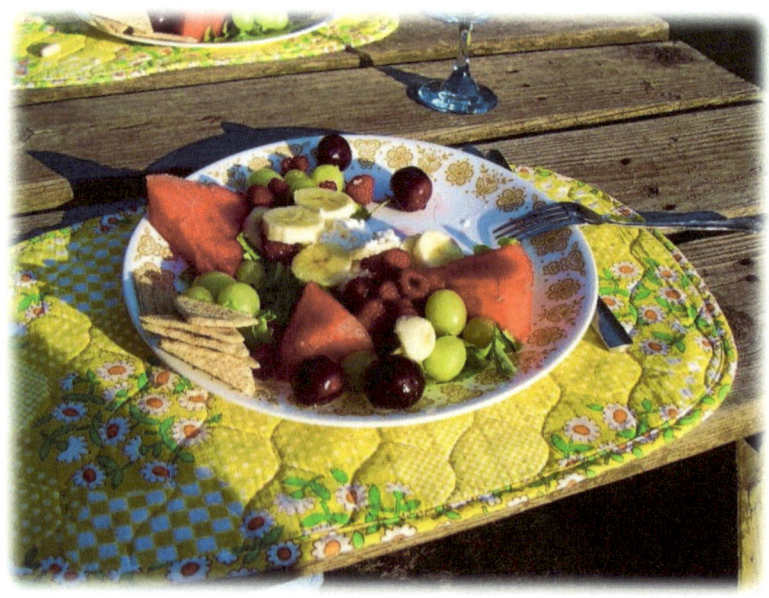

A Summer Supper

Beauty has this effect:

You pause at a heart-stopping image.
What makes it different?
Setting, composition, light, color?
You'll never see this scene again,
so you linger, like an amateur before a
Michelangelo.
You study the way the sun illumines everything,
like the first day of creation:
The intense blue sky,
wispy clouds,
Queen Anne's Lace poking through the needles of a
blue spruce,
rusty wheelbarrow leaning upon the weathered
wood shed,
maroon and gold corn tassels,
caramel dog who wonders why you've stopped
playing with him,
blue and purple butterfly on the thistle,
green, everywhere,
yellow farmhouse with green trim,
and the faded blue curtains in the windows.

That's not all.
There's the coo of the dove you've startled
and the smell of sated earth after the rain.
You're reluctant to leave.
You want to recall this beauty
before returning calls, reading e-mail, fixing supper.

The God Particle

I found the "God Particle" physicists seek
while looking out over a canyon where
condors soar, high in the Peruvian Andes.
While gazing, I also found myself.

I found the God Particle
in the tiny barn owl perched
six feet away. It stared unblinking
and set me straight,

In the juvenile buck,
his antlers, just velvet knobs.
He passed by my window,
leaving courage,

In my small breasts, that,
after my son's birth,
became pillows of milk
that nourished him.

In spritely white June flowers
with genetic instructions to become
sweet red raspberries
for my morning cereal.

In water from underground rivulets
that emerges a cold clean stream
quenching all nature on its way
to the Mississippi and the Gulf of Mexico.

In last year's tomato seeds,
saved and dried through winter,
in their shoots, vines, yellow flowers,
and in their plump red fruit.

In towhees, doves, sparrows,
juncos, chickadees and chipmunks that
dine together under the feeder
no talk of sex, politics or religion.

In the river from devastation
to forgiveness,
healing comes
after despair.

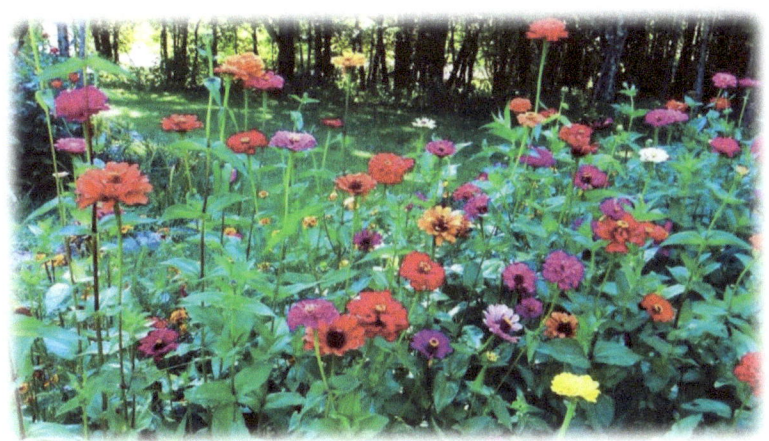

Zinnias

Creation

As I was relaxing on our side porch, an iridescent green hummingbird hovered six inches from my right knee. Then it darted from flower to flower, poking its specialized, long beak into the delicate yellow centers of each red impatiens in the box at my feet. I remained immobile, transfixed by this moment of grace. The hummingbird was the major player, I, the observer, afraid to move even my eyes lest she dart away. I believe in the God who created this perfectly designed creature, and I believe the gifts of nature are manifestations of God's existence.

Orange and yellow jewelweed, for example, sparkle with dew on my morning walks. A fat bee inserts her entire body into the orchid-shaped flowers, her bright yellow pollen sacks bulging. Bulging, too, are the jewelweed seed pods, ready to burst with a tiny pinch from a toddler's fingers. The seeds that fly out, propelled by the tightly wound coil within the pod, never fail to evoke shrieks and laughter from a child, or a world-weary adult.

Rhubarb spreads its rhizomes under our untended garden–the same rhubarb that a farmer's wife planted over a century ago. I continue her tradition, blending the rhubarb in my pies with peach, strawberry, or blackberry. The droops of blackberries burst with sweet wine juices as my husband picks, and I preserve their essence in delicate magenta jelly. As if this bounty were not enough, purple asters (that are really blue) and goldenrod dress the land in my favorite combination of primary colors.

The first time I saw Japanese lanterns, classified as ground cherries because of the shiny round berries within, I thought someone had played a trick on me, sowing the meadow behind our house with fake, outrageously orange flowers that resembled the paper Oriental lanterns used in celebrations.

Closed gentian, with its royal blue tubular flowers is flagrantly regal, its lobes hiding the promise within. Thoreau wrote of "faith in a seed." I know what he meant. This autumn, as days grow shorter, as chlorophyll breaks down in the sugar maple leaves, and they turn from dark green, to orange and yellow, I'm reminded that I'll be a year older when we return next summer; that our returning is related to the safety of this increasingly vulnerable planet, and to the recognition by those in power that it's not only human life at stake when we fail to observe, protect, and partake in the pleasures and wonders of nature, it is the survival of the hummingbird, the wild flowers, the bees, and all those miracles of creation that elicit appreciation and wonder in us, those qualities that make us human.

Despite our apprehension, my husband and I will anticipate our return to Montezuma, to the Appalachian mountains, and to the arrival of our grandchildren so that, once again, they can pinch the seed pods of jewelweed and laugh at the surprise within. In this mountain oasis, I have no doubts about God's existence. I believe in evolution, and I believe in its Designer.

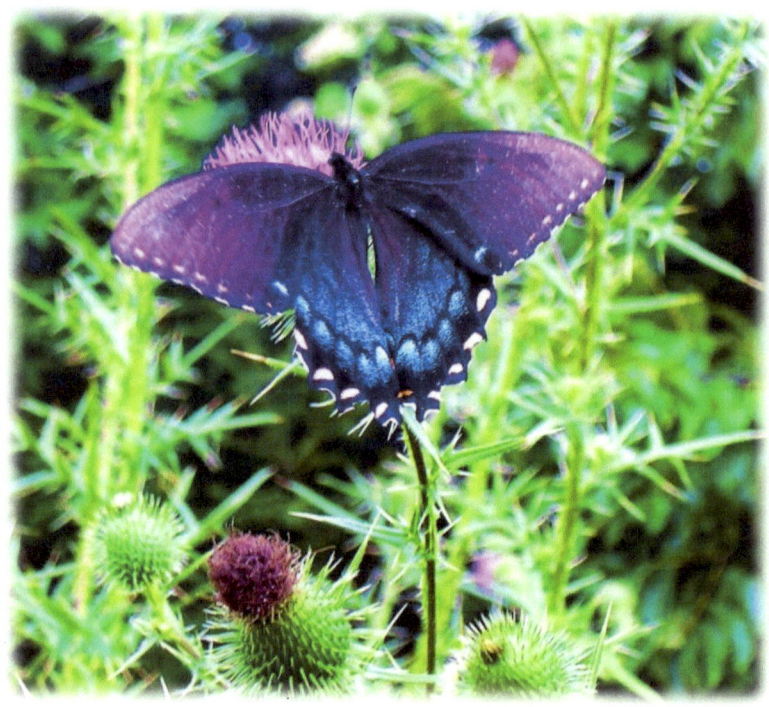

Limenitis arthemis, Red-spotted Purple Butterfly on Thistle

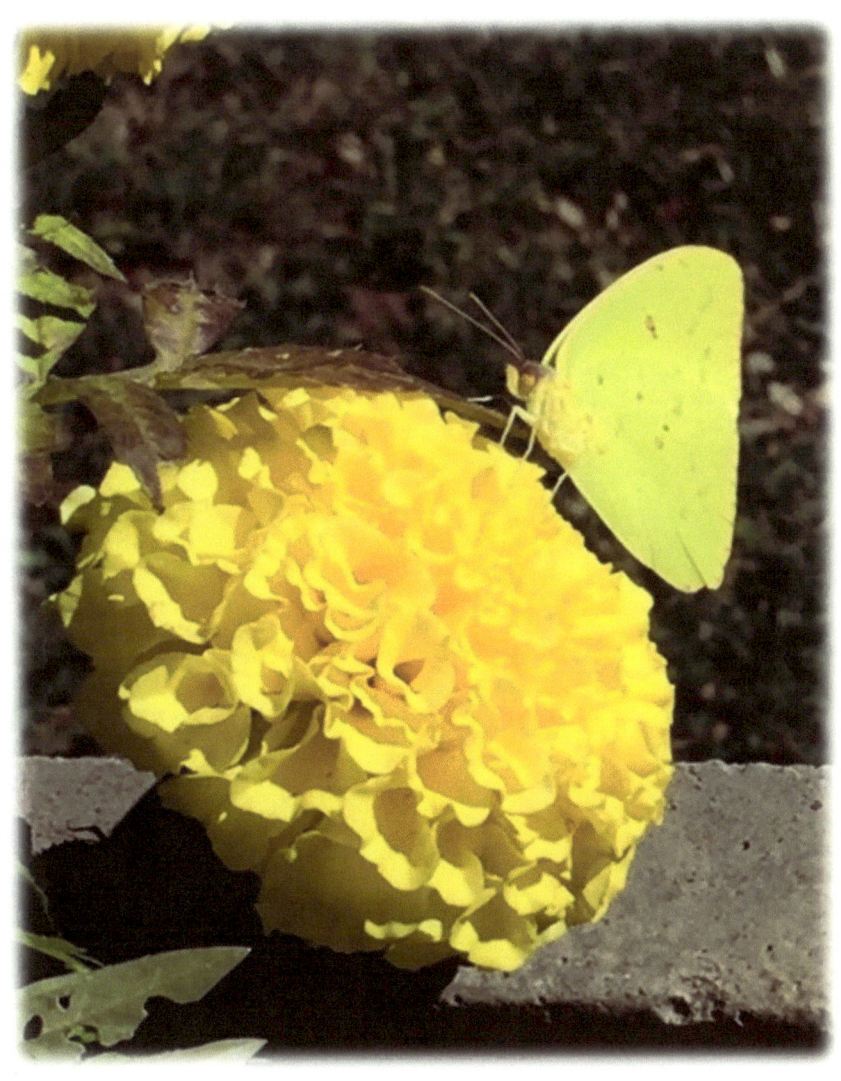

Eurema lisa, Little Sulphur Butterfly

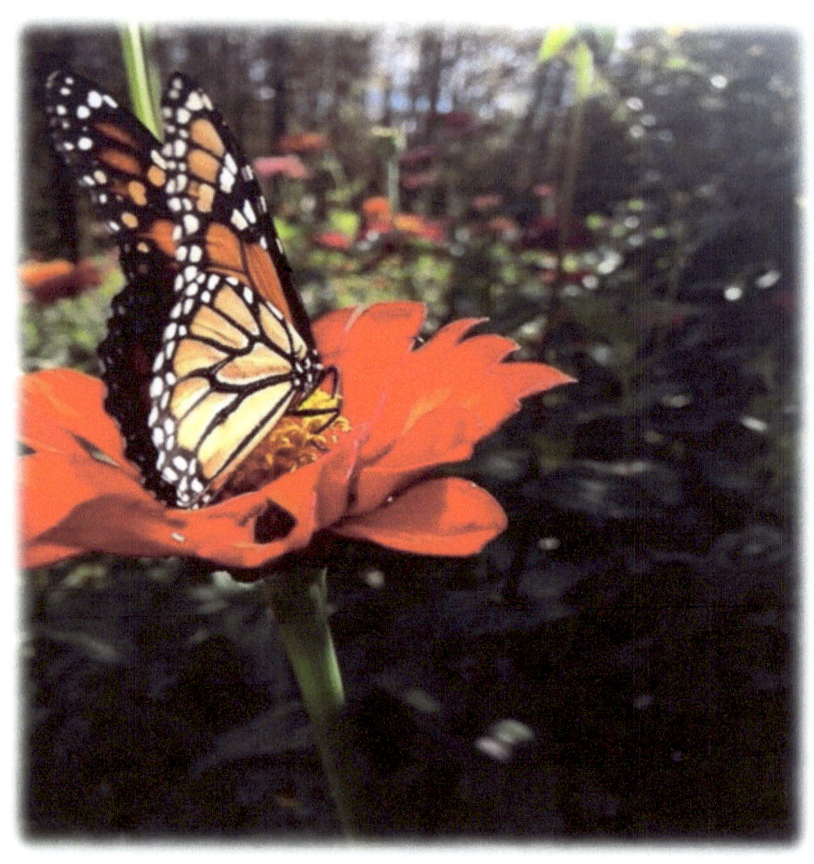

Danaus plexippus, Monarch

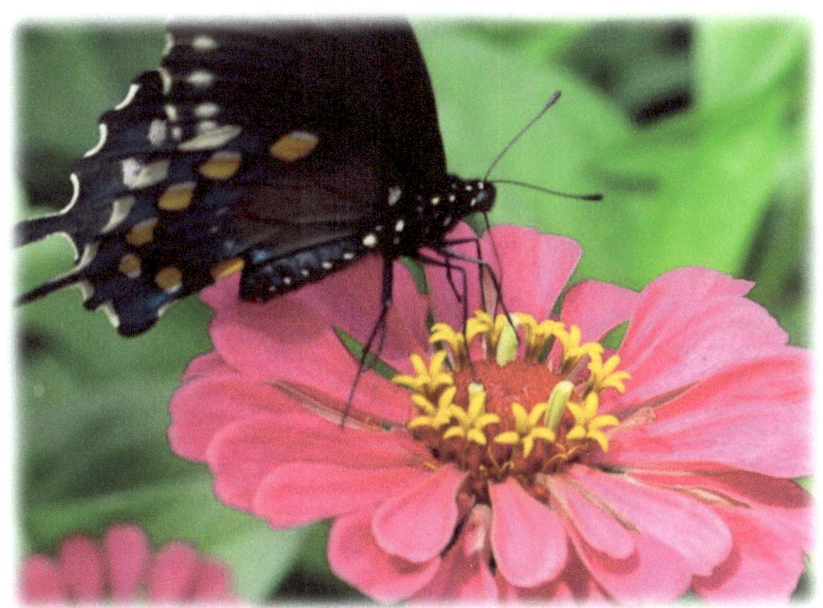

Limenitis arthemis, Red-spotted Purple

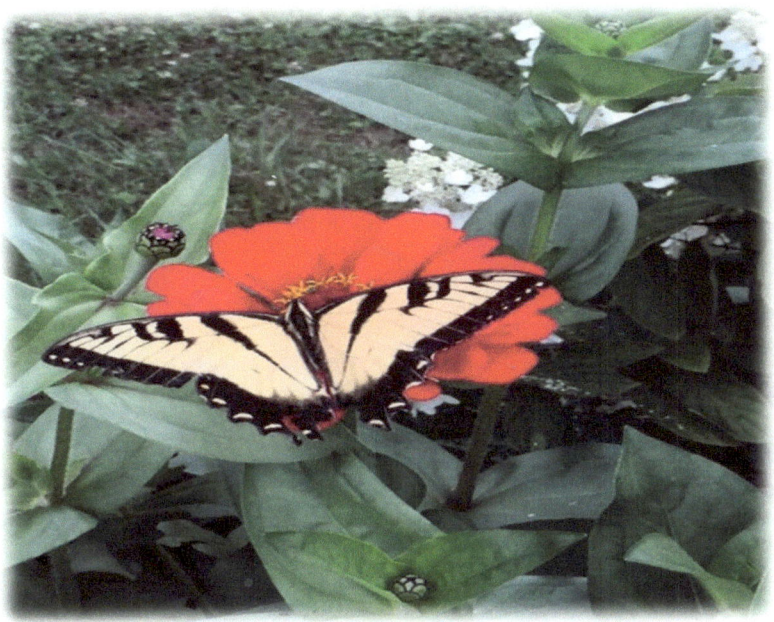

Papilio glaucus, Eastern Swallow Tigertail

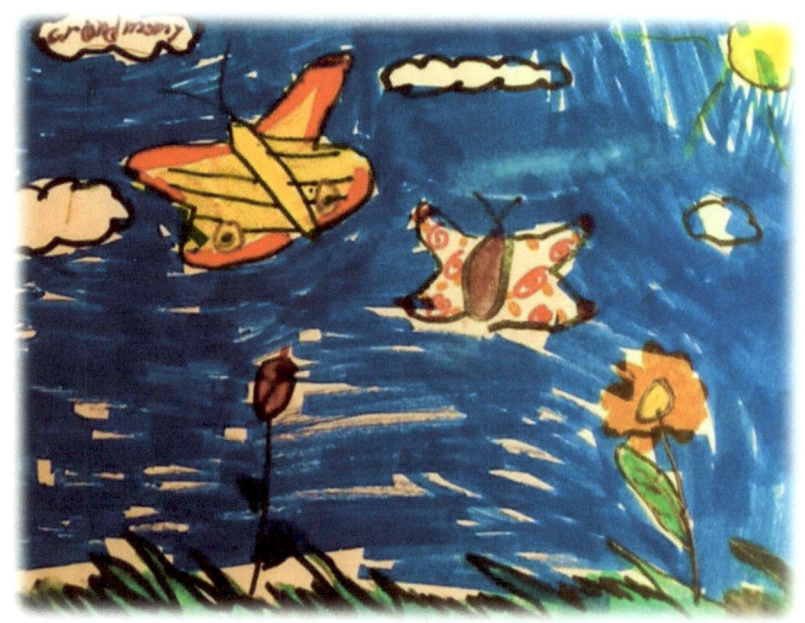

A Granddaughter's Butterflies

Fall

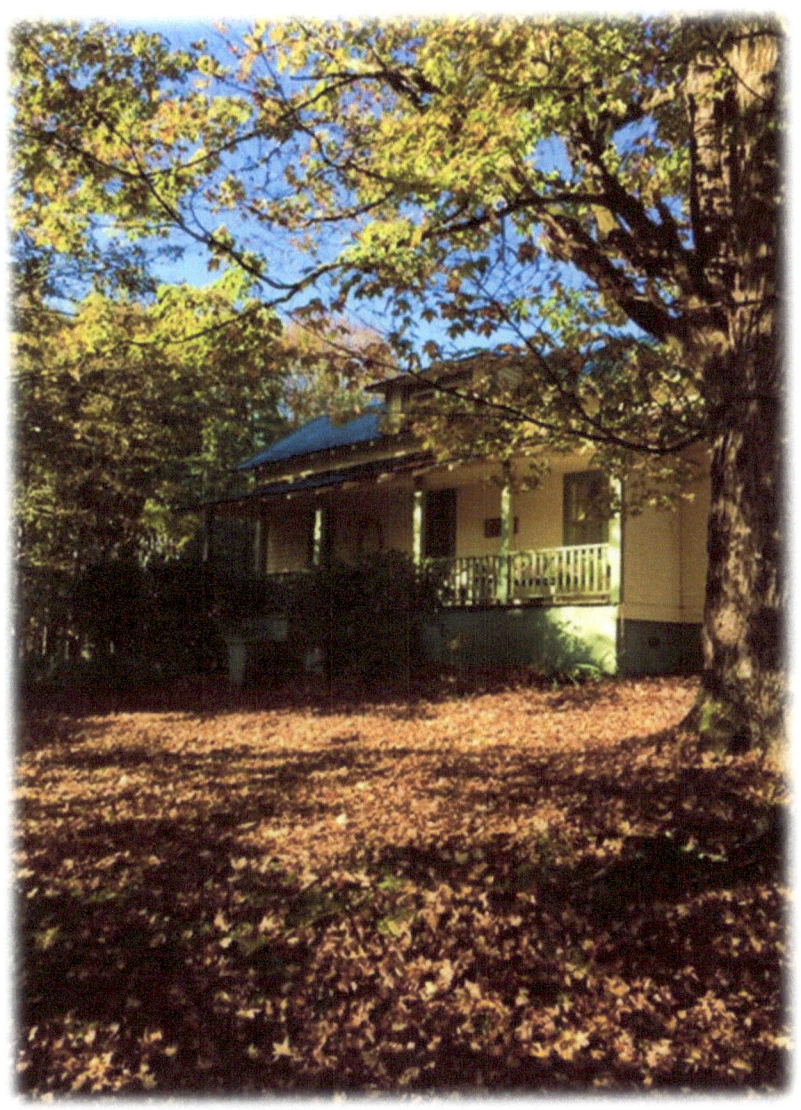

Montezuma's Reward

You Could Die on Such a Day

You could die on such a day
and it would be all right.
You'd close your eyes and see
Just what you're seeing now:

Trembling gold maple leaves
against a cornflower sky,
a vase of plush pink dahlias
the color of babies' lips
on a gray splintered picnic table.
I'm not reaching when I say
the grass is Kelly green
before the first frost smacks it down, flat and brown.

The honking of geese announces
their flight to warmer climes.
They don't guess at the years that remain.
They do what they must.

Autumn

Stubborn leaves cling to red oak boughs,
resisting the suck of the wind,
their taffeta hymn rebuffing a fate
that will pull them down stream,
around rocks, in whirling eddies, to obscurity.

I could take some home,
press them between the pages
of a thick, musty book.
They'd be found after my death.
"Who put them here?" someone would ask.

The ancient apple trees have lost their leaves
but freeze-dried bittersweet berries hang from their
limbs like dime-store pop beads.
The trunks wear mint-green lichens,
lacy lingerie for their dowagers' humps.

A lethargic fly climbs the green frosted vase
that holds orange Japanese lanterns.
He ascends, unaware that,
in a day or two, he will be dead,
legs up, on a sunny windowsill.

Fall Break

"What's the matter, Mom?" he gently asks,
long limbs lopped over the sofa's arm.
I'm just happy you're home," I reply.
He heard me cry from pain of love.

When he was small, I'd ask him
what he wanted to do when grandpa came.
"Eat him up," he'd say.
Now I want him back in my womb,
safe from traffic, bars, and women.

Autumn Rose

The last yellow rose
bends to autumn winds,
submits and kisses the soil.
Its drying petals become compost
for next year's daughter buds,
fed by their mother's sacrifice.

Smokey's Dying

You pulled your haunches
up the hillside and down the ravine
into a nest of woven rhododendron
that nestled your bloodied gray fur
and delicate feline bones.
Better this, than a cold steel table
and lethal injection.

A Gnarled Apple Tree.

A gnarled apple tree, a Golden Grimes,
grips the soil in the old orchard
where it has withstood onslaughts
since having been planted in 1896
by farmer Abe.

I will use the feminine pronoun:
She has been split and charred by lightning,
battered by wind, scorched by sun,
maimed by ice,
and hollowed by age.

A twisted bare limb no longer feels
the wounds, but the rest of her,
oh…, the rest of her…,
dances to the seasons, hosting bees in spring,
birds in summer, and deer in fall,
when her fruit-heavy boughs drop their tart treasure,
age, no obstacle.

Gold

Marigolds in burnt sienna, orange and yellow.
Caramel dog asleep in the sun.
Yellow bumble bee with orange nectar sack.
Tomatoes, with coral blush.
Maple trees dripping gold bouillon.
Husband's hands, tan, with brown age spots.
This golden moment disappears as I write.

The Sun on my Back

On this cool, autumn afternoon,
the sun penetrates my bare back,
through the skin, muscle, bone,
burning my nostalgic heart.

Looking up from reading *The Paris Wife*,
about Hemingway's first lady,
I see the orange Japanese lanterns
in a brown bottle on the kitchen windowsill.

On the house, above the window,
is a large wreath of bittersweet,
woven by my husband, whose strong hands
cultivate earth and make art.

Above me a bird, whose song
I don't recognize and, nearby,
the papery kisses of maple leaves
as they meet the grass.

My Heart Stretches

Edna St. Vincent Millay wrote,
"Oh world, I cannot hold thee close enough."

On this autumn day, as apples hoard the last of
summer sun, my heart stretches to breaking.

I warm myself by the fire before grinding coffee
and putting on the oatmeal,

witness the subtle tinting from green to orange
to yellow in the sugar maple grove,

burnish a buckeye on my jeans, till it glows
a warm mahogany,

hear brook water as it breaks upon rocks before
crystals of hoar frost replace jewelweed on the bank,

feast on the vision of purple asters and goldenrod,
the primary colors of September,

smell the dried leaves I crush underfoot, no
difference
now between maple, oak, beech, birch.

The yellow and red bittersweet berries
punctuate my life.

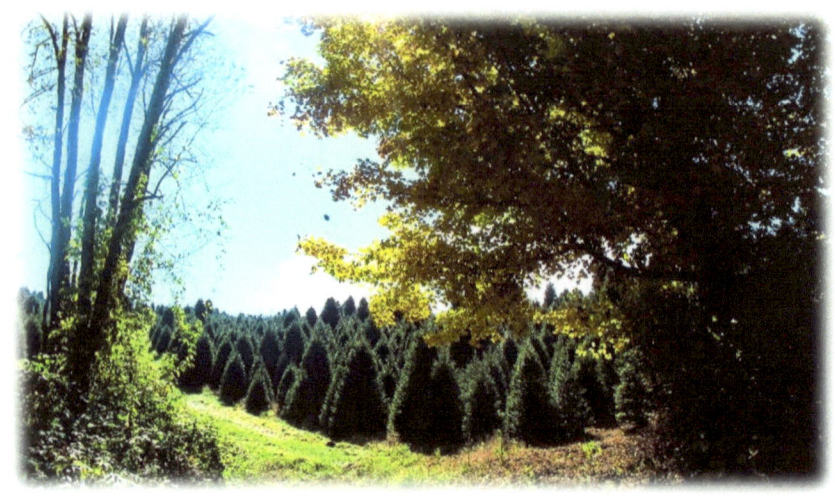

Fraser firs

From Christmas Trees to Chestnut Trees

For many years we raised Fraser firs, *Abies fraseri*, on our land. The tree, native to the Appalachian mountains of the Southeastern United States, is known for its beautiful shape, needle retention, dark blue-green color, fragrance, and its hardiness for shipping. Because of these qualities, it is known as the "Cadillac" of Christmas trees. Chances are that, when you go looking for your live tree after Thanksgiving, you may visit a lot that features Fraser firs from North Carolina.

Given our seven-month yearly absence from the land, it was easier for us to lease the land to a nursery than for us to try to raise the trees ourselves. The employees, mostly immigrants from

Mexico and Central America, came every few weeks to trim the trees with their *machetes*, forming the perfect shape we've come to expect in the classic Christmas tree.

We should have been paying closer attention to the working conditions of the laborers as well as to the pesticides and herbicides they were using. Those chemicals were killing the wild flowers that grew among the trees and damaging the soil. Eventually we noticed that it was eroding because there was no plant life to anchor it. The rain formed small gullies all over the slopes through which rain surged, carrying the soil with it. And, when we had no rain, the sun parched the soil. The brown-eyed Susans, daisies, purple asters and goldenrod stopped growing and the bees and gold finches stopped visiting.

One day a truck carrying workers and spray equipment drove up our driveway and parked next to our house. The men proceeded to unload their equipment and lug it up to the land behind the house where they began to spray the trees and soil between the trees. I noticed that the wind was blowing the chemicals back onto the workers who had no masks or protective clothing. Holding a cloth over my mouth and nose, I approached one of the workers, and, in Spanish, asked for his *jefe*. The boss had left. I asked the men to stop working and phoned the boss, telling him to retrieve the men and not to come back until they had protective gear. That was the end of our Christmas tree endeavor, but we still have a number of towering "Cadillac" trees, fit for the White House.

My husband put in chestnut seedlings to take the place of the Fraser firs. In the early years of our country, this part of North Carolina was covered in chestnut trees, some with enormous girths. According to the web site of the American Chestnut Foundation,

"...there were "nearly 4 billion American chestnut trees growing in the eastern U.S. They were among the largest, tallest, and fastest-growing trees. The nuts fed billions of birds and animals. It was almost a perfect tree, that is, until a blight fungus killed it more than a century ago. The chestnut blight has been called the greatest ecological disaster to strike the world's forests in all of history."

Fortunately, scientists continue trying to preserve the positive qualities of the American chestnut by hybridizing them with a small amount of disease-resistant DNA from the Chinese chestnut. We planted such a variety. And now, twelve years after planting, our trees have grown to impressive heights, and their wide canopies provide rich shade, providing shelter for birds and squirrels who await October when the burrs turn from green to brown, gradually open, and release their nuts. It's our pleasant task to go out with our baskets and harvest nuts for our family and friends before the squirrels and chipmunks get to them. What a treat it is to roast and eat them hot. And the best part? No pesticides or herbicides needed. Not a drop.

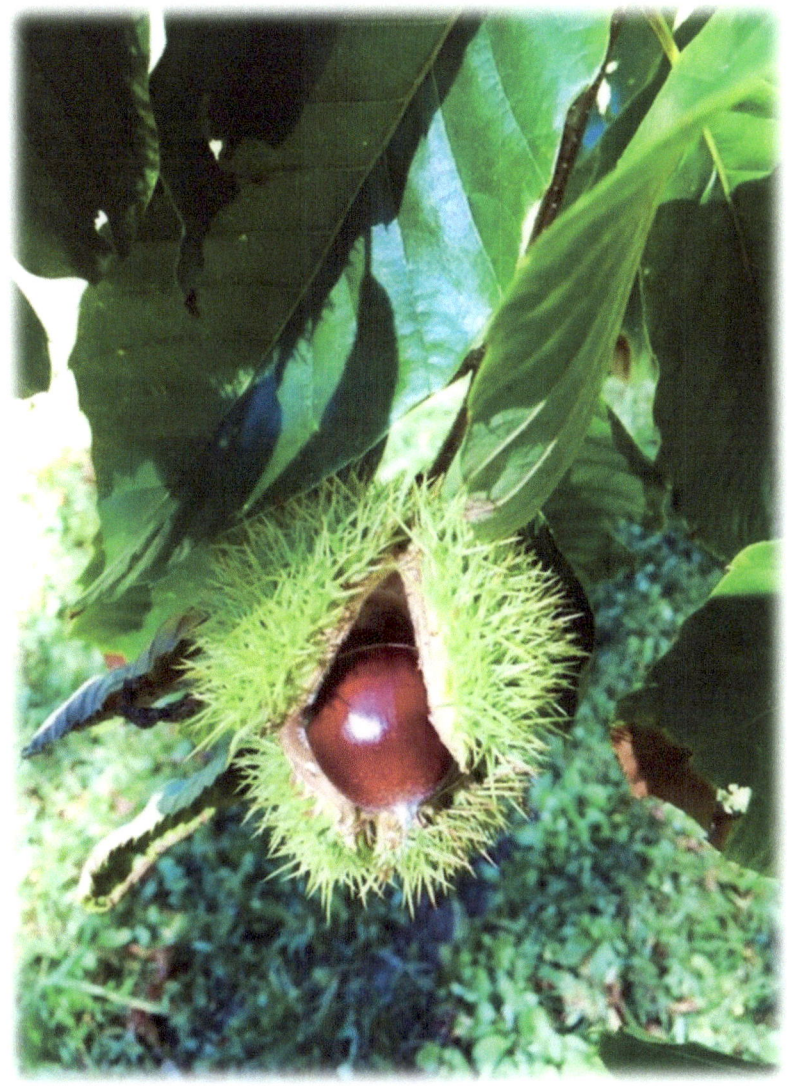

Birth of a Chestnut

Migration South

Lows in the 30s tonight,
snow flurries at the higher elevations.
I pick the last of the tomatoes,
leaving the zinnia seeds to dry
a little more before harvesting
in preparation for next summer's
riotous display.

Red rose hips droop from the trellis.
The dog who adopts us each summer
curls up in the dwindling sun.
Smoke curls from our chimney.
"Our house," I think, "our lives."
So many generations, nameless now,
grew up in this old place.

Snow will soon quilt the garden,
but we know what lies below:
The DNA of corn,
all manner of vegetables,
and lots of flowers.
One day our ashes will be here too,
where the ferns grow, down near the stream.

Today the postmistress said it's time to change our address.

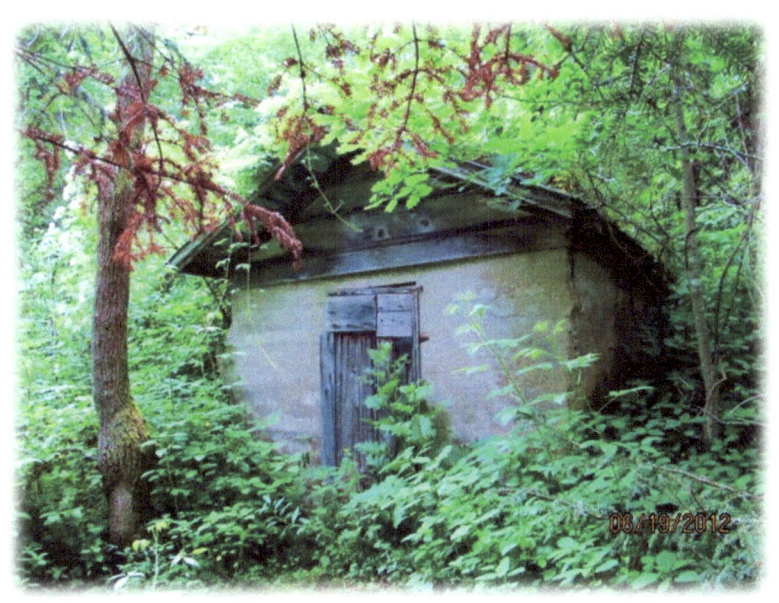

Root Cellar

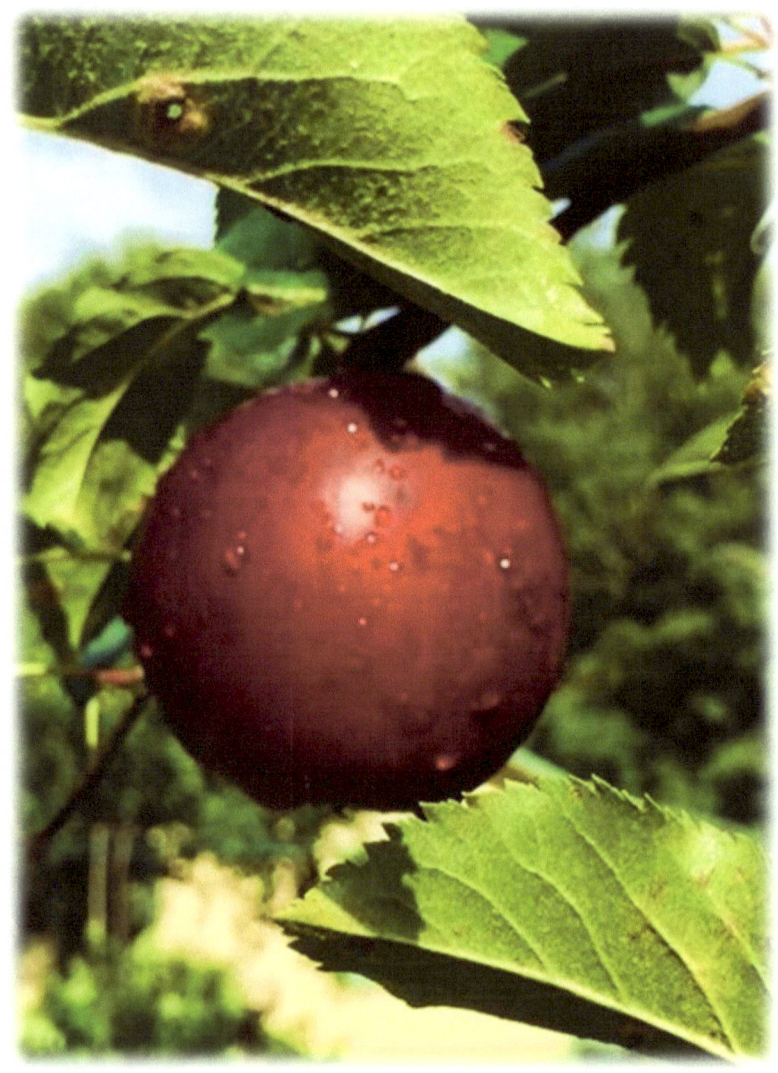

Temptation

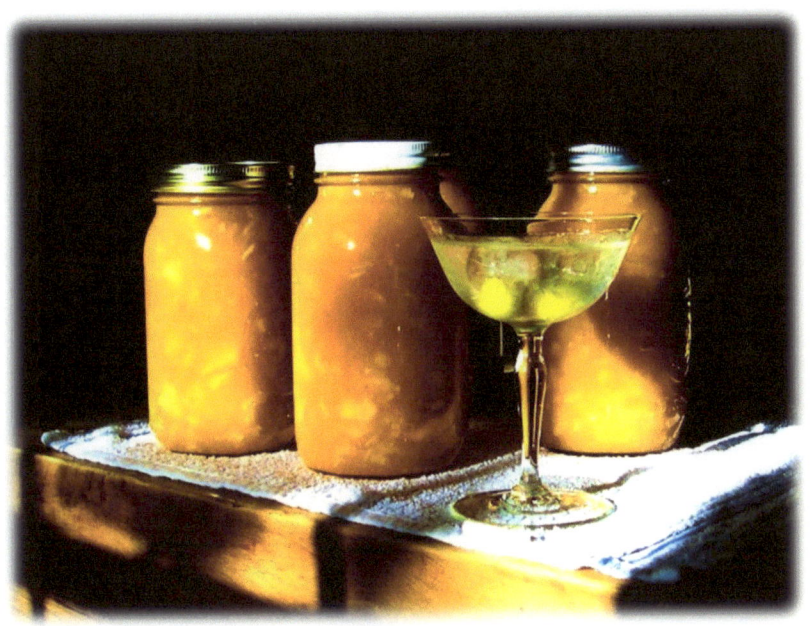

Apple Sauce and Martini

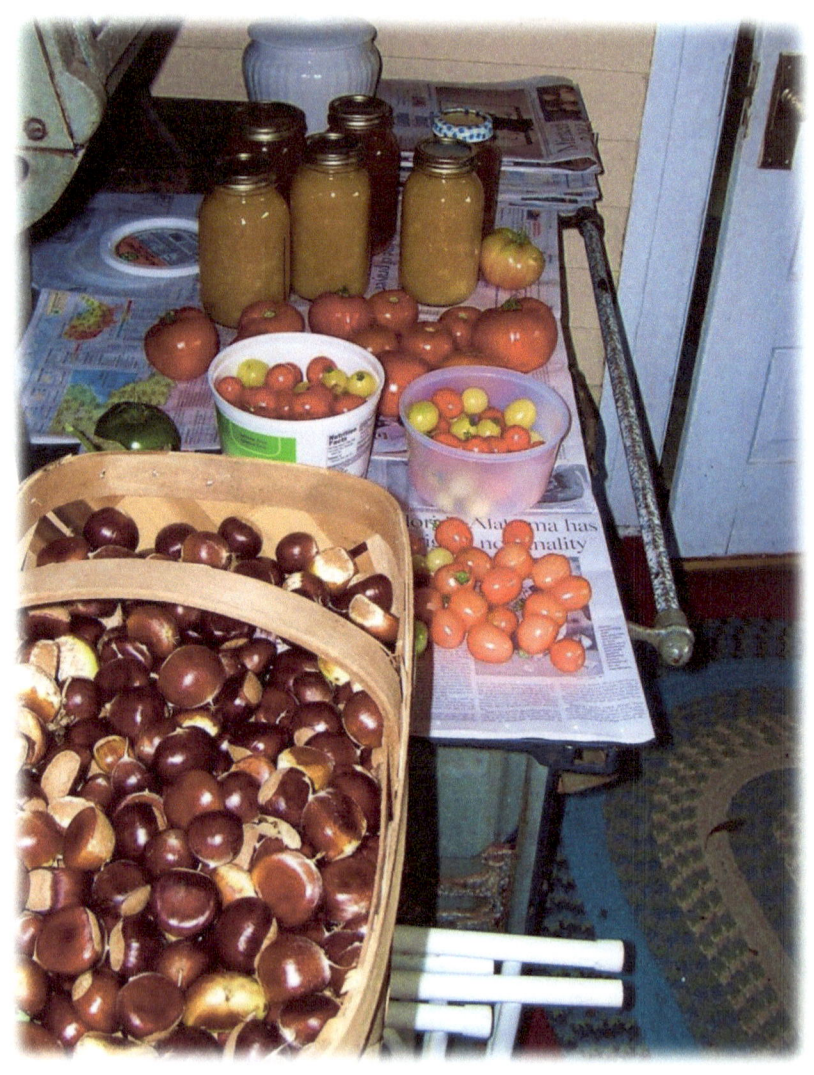

Abundance in the Spring House

Winter

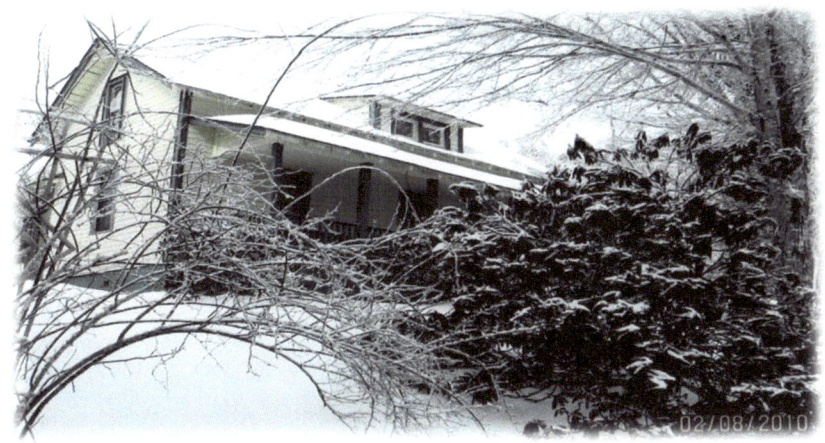

Snowbound

Snowy Morning

The tractor is stored in the tool shed,
reminder of human activity to come.
The only animate creature is a brilliant cardinal
that lights on the bird feeder, its feathers dusted
with snow.

The present, so grimly portrayed by talking
 heads who speak of climate change, extinctions
and violence of all sorts, is out there,
beyond the spruce, apple, and chestnut trees.

The future, the years that remain, my health,
the circumstances of my death are also hidden.
I live with the questions on this snowy morning
and am at peace.

The Yellow House Coat

As the snow falls, light as the
lace on the collar, she mends the
yellow house coat.
How many times now?
Each time, she sees herself
bent over a crib,
smiling at her baby,
wearing this soft, welcoming
son dress.

The threads unravel
like the years.
A new rent appears
but she won't discard it.
Holding it, her belly swells
and her breasts fill.
She is twenty-eight.
Her arms await.

Winter, a Quieter Beauty

When Joe and I were younger we would frequently drive up to Montezuma after Christmas, a good ten to eleven-hour drive from Pensacola, depending upon traffic in and around Atlanta. We wanted to see the snow, hunker down next to the wood-burning stove, and enjoy the solitude of our farmhouse after the razzle dazzle of the holiday season.

There is no central heat (or air conditioning) in "Montezuma's Reward," however, and, having been built in 1886, there is no insulation, although we have found crushed newspapers from the 1920s stuffed, like chinking, between boards in the attic, re-purposed to accommodate two bedrooms.

When you enter the spring house through the side door, you smell the apples that have been stored there each season. Once inside the bright yellow kitchen, a peace comes over you before you start to shiver from the inside out because your bones feel like icicles. A scene from the movie "Dr. Zhivago" comes to mind: Lara (Julie Christie) and Dr. Zhivago (Omar Shariff) enter his family's *dacha*, or country house, during the middle of a fierce Russian winter. In the scene, just like here, every window is etched with frost, and they see their breath as do we.

Joe heads out to the woodshed, shovels out the snow that has drifted against its door, gathers wood he has split the previous year, and builds a fire in the family room stove. Even though I grew up in Wisconsin, my years in Florida have made me a useless, stone-cold statue. I sit shivering next to the stove until thawing occurs. Only then am I ready to set up the kitchen, remove the sheets covering the well-worn furniture, and make the beds.

    Back in Pensacola, I recall, with sweet nostalgia, the board games, snowball fights, and the ski gear drying before the fire while hot toddies warmed the adults. Alas, the preparations we would make to leave in fall—the winterizing of the plumbing, draining the hot water heater, etc.—became too much to un-do for a week's stay in winter only to be re-done before our return to warmer weather.

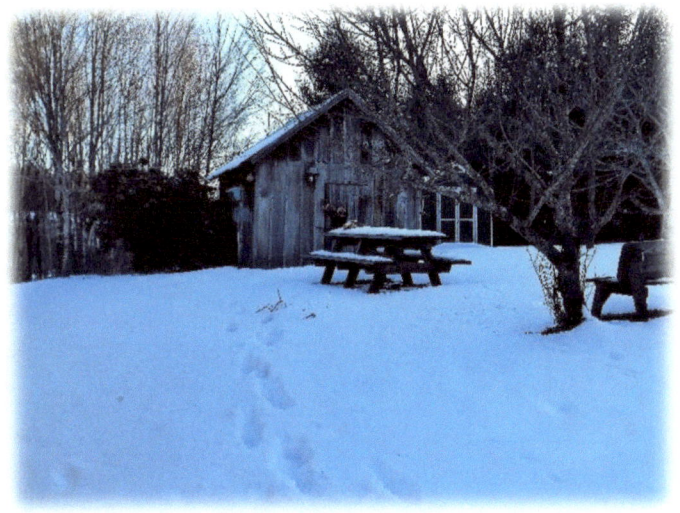

Backyard at Dusk

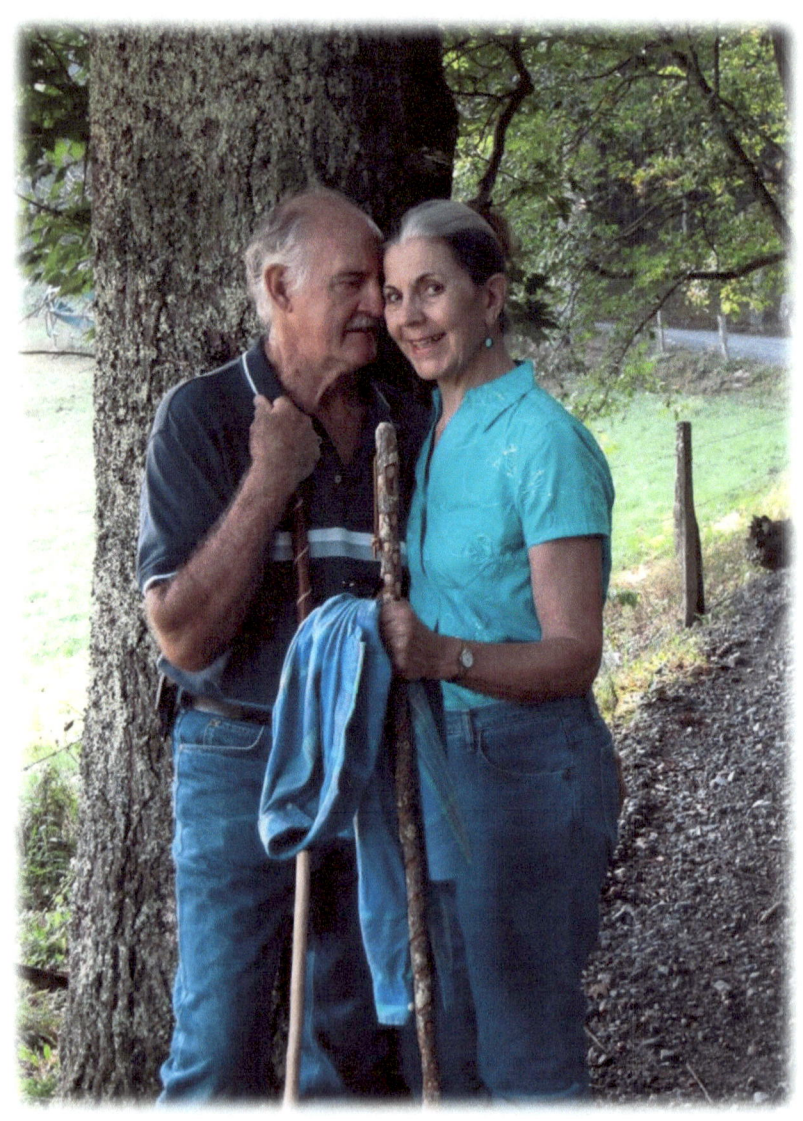

Author and Husband on Old Montezuma Road

About the Author

Patricia was born and raised in Milwaukee, Wisconsin. After working as a speech therapist in rural Wisconsin schools, she joined the Peace Corps and headed to Peru for two years where she worked in the area of public health. Later, upon completion of her master's degree and doctorate, she joined the University of West Florida in Pensacola where she enjoyed a long teaching career, ultimately serving as director of International Education and Programs. She has written extensively about the relationship between social conditions and democracy and has been a United Nations consultant to women's groups in Peru and Brazil.

www.patriciaedmistenbooks.com

Acknowledgement:

With special thanks to Susan Lewis of Proper Publishing for the patience and skill she demonstrated during the formatting of this book.

If you would like to order any of Patricia Edmisten's books, they are available for purchase on Amazon Worldwide.

If you would like an inscribed copy of this book, you can contact her at:

pedmisten@uwf.edu

www.ingramcontent.com/pod-product-compliance
Lightning Source LLC
Chambersburg PA
CBHW040228220526
45473CB00001B/164